Paleo Diet

Beginners and seniors cookbook, paleolithic recipes for weight loss, and to live a healthy and whole-foods lifestyle.

Donald T Praise

Table of Contents

INTRODUCTION

Are you among the set of people who've made up their mind to lose fat and stay young and fresh, while avoiding cancer, diabetes, heart disease, Parkinson's, Alzheimer's and lot of other illnesses?

Paleo diet is a diet that encompass wholesome, nutritious, paleo-approved recipes your body need to feel the mightiest benefits attached to the paleo diet for a better lifestyle.

This guide will give you the information to gain the knowledge and wisdom in order to succeed and make your goals more realistic. through "what and what not to eat" to give you the optimum best just as tucking into a delicious Spinach Frittata for breakfast, a Paleo Salmon Pie for lunch or Sausage Casserole for dinner. Those are just some of the delicious meals you could be preparing and enjoying, along with a range of desserts to treat yourself and make you feel motivated during the day.

CHAPTER 1

Get Rid Of Cliff Paleo Diet Plan: The Do's And Don'ts & What Things To Expect

What is a Paleo diet plan?

The Paleo diet plan is dependant on eating foods that could have already been available through the Paleolithic era, which ranged from 2.6 million years back to about 12,000 years back. The diet plan primarily consists of liver organ, seafood, fruit, veggies, nut products, seed products. Essentially, food items that could have easily become acquired by searching and collecting. The dietary plan will be furthermore generally known as the Paleolithic diet plan, Rock Age group diet plan, hunter-gatherer diet plan, or caveman diet plan.

What can you take in on the Paleo diet plan?

Here's a fast listing of meals you May consume on the
Paleo diet plan:

- Grass-fed Meat

- Seafood

- Fruits

- Vegetables

- Eggs

- Nuts

- Seeds

Healthful oils (such as olive, walnut, flaxseed, macadamia,
avocado, and coconut).

Destroy Cliff beverages...indeed, seriously, they are all organic and contain Paleo compliant ingredients.

So what can you not eat on the Paleo diet plan?

Here's a fast checklist of food items you can't consume on the Paleo diet plan:

- Grains (such as whole wheat, oats, and barley)

- Dried beans (nuts, coffee beans, lentils, tofu)

- Refined sugar & synthetic sweeteners

- Dairy products

- Salt

- Potatoes

- Prepared foods

What may We beverage on the Paleo diet plan?

Pure, filtered water is among your finest choices. It won't end up being filled up with any harmful chemical substances if strained correctly. Also, it won't consist of chlorine-like plain tap water.

Pure fruits or veggie juice can be an excellent option if you are searching for some additional taste in your beverage. Nevertheless, avoid proceeding purchase of any juice from the grocery store shop, as much of the normal fruit juices are usually packed with synthetic sugar. Your very best wager would be to buy a juicer and your preferred fruits & vegetables at home.

Espresso is not permitted on the Paleo diet plan, but one of the primary benefits of the dietary plan is that you balance your blood sugar levels by providing proteins and fat-rich foods, so you might get that it's not necessary espresso. Espresso is usually a by-product of individuals not really getting steady bloodstream sugars, consequently getting reduced power.

Alcoholic beverages are not technically prohibited from the Paleo diet plan, nevertheless, you must not be binge taking in on the dietary plan. Individuals and creatures have already been eating fermented meals and beverages for a long time. Nevertheless, an excessive amount of alcoholic beverages may not give you a wonderful (but occasionally preferred) ale stomach and hit your cholesterol amounts off-kilter, therefore you need to be conscious of just how much you are usually taking in. It could be well worth using the award-winning GUTEN beverage to consider your caveman methods up a level.

Soda pops, energy beverages, and sports activities beverages are usually almost all filled up with artificial sweeteners, thus definitely avoid them throughout a Paleo diet plan. Once again, natural and organic beverages with

Paleo-compliant components can be taken, therefore be sure to check out Wipeout Cliff beverages that fit the bill for any fix, suffered overall performance, or recuperation.

Why Paleo is usually harmful to you?

Within the short-term, a Paleo is not harmful to you due to the fact that you're consuming clean food and steering clear of processed sugars, artificial sweeteners, sodium, and processed food items. The diet program will most likely result in weight reduction or at the very least maintain your excess weight.

It ought to be noted that we now have zero long-term clinical research on the advantages and possible risks of the Paleo diet plan. Although extensive ramifications of consuming plenty of meals filled up with synthetic sugar and sodium are usually most likely very much even worse compared to the long-lasting ramifications of a Paleo diet plan, you should be cautious and consult with a clinical expert if you're going through severe unwanted effects.

Can you shed weight on the Paleo diet plan?

Yes! The dietary plan strategy in a Paleo diet plan might help you shed weight in several various methods.

The Paleo diet plan is normally high in proteins. Proteins can be an essential nutritional in weight reduction as it could boost your metabolic process, lower your hunger, and handle many of the bodily hormones that regulate your bodyweight.

What things to expect when feeding on Paleo?

When you start the diet plan, you'll likely see fast weight

loss from about 5 to 10 lbs within the initial week. Though that is motivating, it's mainly simply water pounds. You can't get frustrated at these times as you'll nevertheless shed weight in case you adhere to the diet plan.

After your initial drop in weight, you'll likely visit a slow and steady pace of weight reduction. The regular weight reduction is all about one or two lbs weekly.

Which are the part results of the Paleo diet plan?

Like any significant diet plan switch, a Paleo diet plan will likely result in unwanted effects as the body adapts towards the modifications. This is a set of the feasible aspect of results of the Paleo diet plan:

- Lower blood sugar levels

- Cravings

- Absence of power (initially)

- Poor breath

- Switch in bowels

- Low-carb flu

How do you ease right into a Paleo diet plan?

The Paleo diet plan could be a drastic modification in what you eat. There are many methods for you to simply be involved with it.

Modification, the sort of skin oils a person makes use of - Feed and seeds skin oils are usually terrible for you personally. Changing to natural oils such as grass-fed butter, coconut essential oil, and further virgin essential olive oil are usually healthier alternatives that you most likely won't see. Producing this change can help avoid swelling along with other poor unwanted effects.

You can stick to white rice - If you could have heard that brown rice is a lot healthier than white rice, there's no ton of proof that backs that state. Dark brown grain could end up being even worse for you because of the higher level of phytic acidity it includes, which prevents chemical assimilation. If you like the flavor of the whitened grain, may sense poor about keeping it.

Fruits:- Fruits are usually filled with good nutritional vitamins, dietary fiber, and anti-oxidants. There is also the additional good thing about getting a lesser glucose content material than almost every other fruit. This is not to state that you should not consume any fruit, but be sure to bunch on those fruits within the make area.

Stick to your origins:- Main veggies are usually good for you personally because they are loaded along with nutrition and are usually a good way to get food power.

Outside the apparent types such as celery, onions, and taters, you can find a wide variety of tasty choices like beets, turnips, radishes, and yams merely to title several.

Any Type of efficiency beverages which are Paleo pleasant?

Yes! Getting rid of Cliff can offer the beverages you will need to help keep you ahead throughout your Paleo diet plan without busting the guidelines. All Eliminate Cliff beverages are sweetened normally and not necessarily filled up with the rubbish that a lot of soda pops, energy beverages, and sports activities beverages consist of.

Ignite is our power beverage:- it offers sports athletes having a clear way to obtain Coffee from *Green Tea Extract.* Also, it contains plenty of W Nutritional vitamins, Magnesium, Potassium, and electrolytes that allows a sluggish launch from the coffee avoiding a power accident down the road.

Endure is a specialized mixture of slow-release carb gas (palatinose) and electrolytes to aid hydration and sustained stamina to help you to continue to stay ahead during your exercise.

CHAPTER 2

Paleo diet plan: The facts and why could it be so well-known?

Maybe the Paleo diet plan, a diet modeled on prehistoric human diet plans, befitting contemporary humans?

The paleo diet plan is a diet strategy predicated on meals much like what may have been eaten through the Paleolithic era, which increases from approximately 2.5 million to 10,000 years back.

The paleo diet plan typically includes liver organ, seafood, fruit, veggies, and seed products – previous food items could be obtained by looking and collecting. A paleo diet plan limits meals that grew to be typical when gardening surfaced about 10,000 years back. These food items consist of milk products, dried beans, and grains.

Some other titles for any paleo diet plan include Paleolithic diet plan, Rock Age diet plan, hunter-gatherer diet plan, and caveman diet plan.

Purpose

The purpose of a paleo diet plan is to go back to a means of eating that which is similar to what early human beings ate. The diet's thinking is the fact that our body will be genetically mismatched to the present-day diet plan that surfaced with gardening methods - a concept referred to as the discordance speculation.

Gardening transformed what people consumed and founded dairy products, grains, and dried beans because of extra staples in the individual diet plan. This fairly past due and quick switch in the diet plan, based on the speculation, outpaced your body's capability to adapt. This mismatch will be thought to be an added aspect towards the frequency of unhealthy weight, diabetes, and cardiovascular disease nowadays.

Why you may follow a paleo diet

You might decide to follow a paleo diet plan as you:

- Would like to shed weight or maintain a wholesome weight.

- Want help arranging meals

Information on the paleo diet

Suggestions vary among business paleo diet programs, plus some diet plan programs have got stricter recommendations than others. Generally, paleo diet plans adhere to these suggestions.

Here, take a look at everything you might consume during a common time carrying out a paleo diet plan:

Morning meal. Broiled trout and cantaloupe.

Lunchtime. Broiled slim pig loin and greens (romaine, carrot, cucumber, tomato vegetables, walnuts, and lime fruit juice outfitting).

Supper. Slim meat sirloin suggestion roast, steamed broccoli, salad (combined vegetables, tomato vegetables, avocado, onions, walnuts, and " lemon " juice dressing up), and strawberries for delicacy.

Snack foods. A fruit, carrot, or oatmeal.

The dietary plan also emphasizes normal water and being physically active each day.

Results

Several randomized clinical trials have compared the paleo diet plan to various other diet programs, like the Mediterranean sea Diet plan or the Diabetes Diet plan.

Generally, these tests claim that a paleo diet plan might provide some advantages in comparison to diet programs of fruit, veggies, liver organ, whole grains, dried beans, and low-fat milk products. These advantages can include:

- More excess weight loss

- Enhanced glucose tolerance

- Much better blood circulation pressure control

- Decrease triglycerides

- Much better hunger management

Nevertheless, more studies with large sets of people arbitrarily designated to various diet programs are essential to comprehend the long-term, general health advantages and possible dangers of the paleo diet plan.

Queries about paleo diets

Issues or even queries concerning the paleo diet plan

include both meals choice as well as the underlying speculation.

Diet concerns

The paleo diet plan is abundant with veggies, fruit, and peanuts - all components of a healthy diet plan.

The principal difference between your paleo diet plan with other healthy diet programs is the lack of whole grains and legumes, which are believed to be good resources of fiber, vitamins with other nutrients. Furthermore lacking from the dietary plan are usually milk products, that are good resources of proteins and calcium mineral.

These meals are not merely taken into consideration healthful but also are usually less expensive and available than the like of food items as an outrageous sport, grass-fed animals, and crazy. For a lot of, a paleo diet plan may be costly.

Queries concerning the paleo diet plan hypothesis

Scientists have argued the fact that underlying speculation from the paleo diet plan might oversimplify the storyplot of how people adapted to adjustments in the diet plan. Quarrels to get a more complex knowledge of the development of human dietary requirements are the pursuing:

Variants in diet plan predicated on location, weather, and food accessibility - not merely the changeover to gardening - also could have shaped the advancement of nutritional requirements.

Archaeological research has proven that earlier individual diets could have incorporated crazy grains for about 30,000 years back prior to the introduction of farming.

Hereditary research shows that significant evolutionary changes continue following the Paleolithic era, including diet-related changes, such as an increase in the number of genes linked to the breakdown of nutritional starches.

The paleo diet plan can help you shed weight or even sustain your pounds. It could furthermore have some other advantageous wellness results. Nevertheless, you can find no extensive medical research concerning the advantages and possible dangers of the dietary plan.

You may be in a position to achieve the same health advantages by getting plenty of workouts and feeding on a balanced, nutritious diet with plenty of fruits & vegetables.

CHAPTER 3

Before You Start the Paleo Diet plan

You might have found out about the Paleo diet plan, and still discover some individuals who have had achievement with the program, thus what's the damage in trying it on your own? To start with, the Paleo diet plan, which will be in line with the concept that we ought to eat like our Paleolithic forefathers, will be extremely restrictive. Because of this, it requires cautious arrangement to make sure that the diet plan will be well balanced and offers all the important nutrition we need to remain healthful.

Challenges

The Paleo diet plan is heavy in the pet protein division. This form of consumption promotes the intake of higher quality meat from free-range pets that consume an all-natural diet plan of a lawn. These creatures tend to be leaner than those elevated in focused pet serving procedures (CAFOs) and their meats will be both reduced in condensed excess fat and increased in omega-3 fat such as EPA and DHA. Paleo advocates highlight selecting free-range, grass-fed meat to greatly help lower the quantity of soaked body fat, nevertheless, the condensed extra fat in almost all reddish meats will be greater than that of whitened meats choices like poultry or turkey.

Because the Paleo method of eating removes dairy and dried beans, those sticking with the diet program will probably have a lesser intake of calcium, dietary fiber, along with other nutrients in abundance in these food groups. Although it is be possible to get this nutrition from Paleo-approved resources, it gives a problem. Those third, consuming design frequently don't obtain plenty of calcium mineral, as it's generally discovered in dairy products like dairy and yogurt, which are removed on the dietary plan. Calcium mineral can be an essential nutrient for bone tissue wellness in addition to appropriate sensors and coronary heart functionality. Milk products, which include Ancient greek yogurt, whole milk, and cheese, may also be good resources of proteins. Those following a diet plan must get calcium mineral from veggies like broccoli or nut products such as walnuts. To greatly help Paleo predators obtain good enough calcium mineral, below is a set of calcium-rich, Paleo-approved food items.

The exclusion of legumes in the Paleo diet may also be problematic since it disqualifies an excellent way of getting fiber from the dietary plan. Without healthful dried beans like dark, kidney, or whitened coffee beans, lentils, soybeans, tofu, and so many more, dietary fiber consumption will be significantly decreased set alongside the diet plan of those who eat these food types. A higher dietary fiber diet plan (20-30g/day time) can lower cholesterol, in addition, to enhance Type 2 diabetes in additional, boosting your dietary fiber intake will be associated with enhancements in blood sugar levels handle and bloodstream fats for those who have Type 2 diabetes. While those following a Paleo method of eating might not get their dietary fiber from this resource, it is expected that their increased intake of vegetables & fruits can help them get to the everyday suggestion.

Planning the Paleo diet

As the Paleo diet does offer quite a few impressive benefits, also, it has quite a few serious challenges, each monetarily and nutritionally, that require to be addressed before deciding to stick to it. Although this diet program stresses fruits and veggies, its concern isn't weight reduction. Meat and nut products can become calorically thick and for that reason result in putting on weight, if consumed in large amounts. A much better suggestion could be to accept particular elements of the dietary plan while becoming pickier about others. For instance, selecting mainly new elements, like the ones that might have been developed by our forefathers, can simply result in an improved consumption of nutrient-rich make. In inclusion, whilst getting more than enough proteins is essential for everybody, prioritizing liver organs like poultry, turkey, or eggs instead of reddish colored meat which is increased in fats, may end up being a wiser option. Whole grains, in addition to dried beans, could be essential resources of dietary fiber and proteins. Also, consuming whole grains and dried beans are also demonstrated to lower cholesterol, producing pleasant improvements to a standard healthy diet design, despite Paleo's prevention of these. Lastly, which includes low-fat or fat-free dairy products in the dietary plan guarantees you'll get sufficient important minerals and vitamins while furthermore adding extra proteins to the dietary plan. Therefore, the Paleo diet plan can certainly end up being wellness advertising when carried out properly and cautiously prepared out.

Quantity of calcium mineral in the helping of Paleo-friendly foods

Suggested Nutritional Allowance for calcium supplement will be 1,000 mg/time for grown-ups 19-50 years.

CHAPTER 4

20 Food Items Which Are Harmful To Your Wellness

It's an easy task to get confused about which food items are usually healthy and which aren't.

You generally need to avoid some food items if you wish to lose weight and stop chronic illnesses.

In this specific guide, healthy alternatives are pointed out whenever probable.

Listed below are 20 meals that are usually unhealthy - although a lot of people may eat them in moderation about special occasions without the permanent harm to their wellness.

1. Sugary drinks

Added sugar is among the most severe ingredients in the present-day diet.

Nevertheless, quite a few resources of sugar are usually even worse than others, and sweet drinks are usually harmful.

When beverage water calorie is consumed, the human brain may finish them up mainly because of meals. Therefore, you might finish up, significantly growing your complete calorie consumption.

When consumed in large quantities, sugars may push insulin level of resistance and it is highly associated with non-alcoholic fatty liver organ illness. It's furthermore connected with numerous severe problems, which include Type 2 diabetes and cardiovascular disease.

Some people think that sugary beverages will be the most fattening facet of the contemporary diet plan and taking them in huge amounts can make you get fat and be overweight.

Consume water, soft drinks, espresso, or even green tea instead. Including a cut of lime to water or soft drinks can offer a burst open of taste.

2. Many pizzas

Pizzas are among the world's hottest rubbish food items.

Many business pizzas are created with harmful substances, which includes highly refined money and heavily processed meats. Pizzas furthermore are commonly incredibly saturated in calories from fat.

Alternatives

Some dining places offer more healthy ingredients. Homemade pizza may also be healthful, so long as you select healthful components.

3. White-colored bread

Many breads are harmful if eaten in huge amounts, as they're created from refined whole wheat, which is lower in fiber and important nutritional requirements and could result in rapid spikes in blood sugar levels.

For those who may tolerate gluten, Ezekiel bread is a superb selection. Whole-grain bread can be healthier than a whitened loaf of bread.

4. Many fruit drinks

Fruit juice is frequently assumed to be healthy. While juice contains some antioxidants and vitamin Chemical, also, it packages higher levels of water glucose. In fact, juice harbors as much sugar as sweet drinks like Cola or Soft drink - or a lot more.

Some fruit drinks have been proven to have health advantages despite their sugar content, such as pomegranate and blueberry juices. Nevertheless, these are highly recommended for occasional dietary supplements, and not for everyday section of your diet.

5. Sweetened breakfast cereals

Breakfast cereals are usually processed cereal grains, such as whole wheat, oats, grain, and hammertoe. They're specifically well-liked by kids and sometimes eaten with dairy. To make them even more palatable, the grains are roasted, shredded, pulped, rolled, or flaked. They're usually higher in additional glucose.

The primary downside of all breakfast cereals is their high

added sugar content. Some are usually sweet and they can also be compare to chocolate.

Choose breakfast cereals that are saturated in fiber and lower in added sugar. Better still, create your oat porridge from scrape.

6. Fried, cooked, or broiled food

Baking, barbecuing, and broiling are usually on the list of unhealthiest cooking food strategies.

Meals cooked in these methods tend to be highly palatable and calorie-dense. Various types of harmful chemical substances furthermore type when meals will be prepared under high temperature.

Included in these are acrylamides, acrolein, heterocyclic amines, oxysterols, polycyclic aromatic hydrocarbons

(PAHs), and advanced glycation finish items (AGEs).

Numerous chemical substances shaped during high-heat cooking have already been connected to an elevated threat of cancer and cardiovascular disease.

To improve your wellbeing, choose milder and healthier cooking food strategies, such as cooking, stewing, blanching, and steaming.

7. Pastries, biscuits, and cakes

Many pastries, biscuits, and cakes are harmful if eaten excessively.

Packed versions are usually produced along with processed sugar, sophisticated wheat flour, and added fat. Shortening, which might be higher in harmful trans excess fat, may also be added. These goodies may be tasty, however, they have minimal important nutritional value, copious calories, and several chemical preservatives.

If you can't avoid delicacy, springtime for Greek yogurt, fruit, or chocolates.

8. German french fries and poker chips

Entire, whitened taters have become healthful. Nevertheless, the same cannot be stated of People from France french fries and poker chips. These foods have become saturated in calories, and it's an easy task to eat extreme amounts. Several research hyperlink Finnish french fries and poker chips to put on weight.

These foods could also contain huge amounts of acrylamides, which are carcinogenic substances that form when potatoes are deep-fried, cooked, or roasted.

Taters are usually ideal consumed boiled, not fried. If you want something crunchy to displace spud potato chips, attempt child celery or nut products.

9. Gluten-free junk food

About one-third of the U.S. populace positively attempts to avoid gluten. However, people usually replace healthy, gluten-containing meals with processed junk food which have been gluten-free. These gluten-free alternative products tend to be higher in sugars and enhanced grains such as hammertoe starch or tapioca starch. These elements may result in quick surges in blood sugar levels and are usually lower in important nutrition.

Choose naturally gluten-free foods, such as natural plant and pet foods.

10. Agave nectar

Agave nectar is a sweetener that's often marketed as healthful. Nevertheless, it's extremely processed and intensely saturated in fructose. Large levels of fructose from additional sweeteners could be completely devastating for wellness. Agave nectar is sometimes increased in fructose than many other sweeteners. Whereas desk sugars are 50% fructose and high-fructose hammer toe syrup around 55%, agave nectar is 85% fructose.

Stevia and erythritol are usually healthy, normal, and calorie-free options.

11. Low-fat yogurt

Yogurt could be incredibly healthy. Nonetheless, nearly all yogurts in the supermarket are usually harmful to you.

They're frequently lower in body fat but packed with glucose to pay for the taste that body fat provides. Quite simply, almost all yogurt has already established its healthful, organic extra fat changed having a harmful component.

Furthermore, many yogurts don't provide probiotic bacteria simply because it's usually believed. They're usually pasteurized, which gets rid of the majority of their germs.

Choose normal, full-fat yogurt which has live life or energetic cultures (probiotics). When possible, purchase types from grass-fed cows.

12. Low-carb junk food

Low-carb diet programs have become well-known.

When you can eat a lot of whole foods on this type of diet plan, you need to look out for processed low-carb substitute items. Included in these are low-carb chocolate pubs and food substitutes.

These foods tend to be ready-made and filled with chemicals.

If you're on the low-carb diet plan, shoot for food items that are naturally lower in carbs, such as eggs, seafood, and leafy green.

13. Snow cream

Glaciers lotion could be great tasting, but it's packed with sugars. This dairy products can be saturated in calories and an easy task to over-eat. On the occasion that you consume it like a delicacy, you're generally adding it together with your regular calorie consumption.

It's achievable to choose healthier manufacturers or even help to make your snow lotion making use of fruit and less glucose.

14. Candy bars

Chocolate bars are usually incredibly harmful. They're saturated in sugars, refined wheat flour, and processed fatty acids while furthermore surprisingly low in essential nutrition. What's more, these goodies will keep you starving due to the method your whole body metabolizes these glucose bombs.

Eat fruit or perhaps an item of high-quality chocolates instead.

15. Prepared meat

Even though natural meat could be healthful and healthy, the same is not correct for processed meats. Research display that individuals that eat processed meat possess a higher danger of numerous serious conditions, including intestinal tract malignancy, Type 2 diabetes, and heart problems. Many of these research are usually an observational in character, and therefore they can't prove that processed meats would be at fault. Nevertheless, the statistical hyperlink will be solid and constant between research.

If you wish to eat bacon, sausages, or pepperoni, make an effort to get local butchers who don't add many unhealthy substances.

16. Prepared cheese

Cheese is healthy in moderation. It's packed with nutrition and individual cut packages all of the nutrition as one glass of dairy. Nevertheless, processed cheese items are nothing beats regular cheese. They're mainly made out of filler injections things that are usually designed to truly have a cheese-like look and consistency. Be sure to go through labeling to verify if your cheese consists of dairy products plus a couple of artificial components.

Eat actual cheese rather. Healthful sorts consist of feta, mozzarella, and new cheeses. Several vegan parmesan cheese options may also be good options.

17. Many junk food meals

In most cases, fast-food chains serve processed foods. The majority of their products are usually mass-produced and lower in nutrition. Despite their low costs, junk food might increase the chances of disease and harm your present wellness. You need to specifically look out for deep-fried products.

Due to installation stress, many fast-food stores have started offering healthy choices.

18. High-calorie espresso drinks

Espresso is packed with anti-oxidants and will be offering many advantages. Particularly, coffee consumers possess a lower threat of severe illnesses, such as Type 2 diabetes and Parkinson's. At the same time, the creamers, syrups, additives, and sugar that are frequently put into coffee are highly unhealthy. These products are simply as dangerous as any sugar-sweetened drink.

Consume bare espresso instead. You can include smaller

amounts of weighty lotion or full-fat whole milk if you wish.

19. Anything with additional sugars or sophisticated grains

It's vital that you avoid - or even at minimum control - meals that contain added glucose, refined grains, and artificial trans fat. These are a number of the unhealthiest but most typical elements in the present-day diet plan. Hence, the significance of reading through brands can't be overstated. This even pertains to so-called health foods.

Shoot for nutrient-dense, whole food items, such as fruits and whole grains.

20. Many ready-made foods

The easiest way to consume healthy and shed weight would be to avoid processed food items whenever you can. Prepared materials tend to be packed with extra salt or sugar.

When you're buying, be sure to go through food brands. Make an effort to bunch your trolley with a lot of vegetables along with other whole meals.

Although the Western diet packs a lot of junk food, it is possible to maintain a healthy diet plan if you pun intended, the processed, high-sugar items mentioned previously.

If you concentrate on whole food items, you'll be well on the way to sensation better and reclaiming your wellbeing.

Also, practicing mindfulness once you eat by hearing your body's cues and watching tastes and textures might help you become more conscious of just how much and everything you eat, letting you achieve an improved partnership with meals.

CHAPTER 5

Can the Paleo Diet plan Help You Shed Weight?

The paleo diet plan is among the most popular diet programs you can think. It includes whole, unprocessed food items and emulates how hunter-gatherers ate. Advocates of the dietary plan believe it could reduce the threat of modern medical issues, pointing out that hunter-gathers didn't face the same illnesses that people nowadays do face, such as being overweight, diabetes, and cardiovascular disease. Many reports show that carrying out a paleo diet can result in significant weight reduction and some health improvements

The paleo diet plan promotes eating whole, unprocessed

animal and plant foods like meat, fish, eggs, vegetables, fruits, seeds, and nuts. It avoids processed food items, sugar, dairy products, and grains, even though some versions of stories from the paleo diet carry out allow options such as dairy and grain.

Unlike most diets, a paleo diet will not involve counting calories. Rather, it restricts the aforementioned food groups, which are usually major resources of calorie consumption in the present-day diet.

Research demonstrates diet plans that emphasize whole foods are much better for weight reduction and general health. They are more filling, have fewer calories, and decrease the intake of processed food items, which are associated with many diseases

5 Methods a Paleo Diet plan Might Help You Shed Weight

The paleo diet plan might help you shed weight in lots of ways. Here are 5 of these.

1. Saturated in Protein

Protein may be the most significant nutrient for weight reduction. It can boost your metabolism, lessen your hunger and handle several bodily hormones that regulate your bodyweight. Paleo diet programs encourage feeding on protein-rich foods such as lean meats, seafood, and eggs. In fact, the common paleo diet offers between 25-35% calories from protein.

2. Lower in Carbs

Cutting your carb intake is among the best methods to lose weight. Over 23 studies also show a low-carb diet plan works more effectively than traditional low-fat diet plans for weight reduction. Paleo diets lessen your carb intake through the elimination of common resources of carbs like bread, grain, and potatoes. You must remember that carbs aren't necessarily harmful to you, but restricting your carb intake may lower your regular calorie consumption and help you to lose weight.

3. Reduces Calorie Consumption

To lose excess weight, you usually need to lower your calorie intake. That's the reason why it's vital that you choose foods which are filling because they can fight hunger and help you to eat less. If you have a problem with hunger, a paleo diet could be ideal for you, since it is incredibly filling up. Research has found that this paleo diet is more filling up than other well-known diets just like the Mediterranean and diabetes diets.

Furthermore, studies show a paleo diet plan could help produce more human hormones that help you with the following meal, such as GLP-1, PYY, and GIP, in comparison to diets predicated on traditional recommendations.

4. Eliminates Ready-Made Foods

The modern diet plan is the main reason obesity is increasing. It encourages taking in highly processed meals, which are filled with calories, lower in nutrients, and could increase your threat of many illnesses.

Many reports have found the increase in the use of ready-made foods that mirrors the increase in obesity.

The paleo diet plan restricts ready-made foods because they weren't available through the Paleolithic time frame.

Instead, it stimulates eating lean resources of protein, fruits and veggies, and healthy fat, which are reduced calories and abundant with nutrients.

5. Eliminates Additional Sugar

Like ready-made foods, eating an excessive amount of added sugar could be detrimental to your bodyweight loss attempts and health generally.

It adds calorie consumption to foods and it is low in nutrition. Not forgetting, higher intakes of added sugar may boost your danger of cardiovascular disease and diabetes.

The paleo diet plan eliminates added sugar altogether and

also promotes natural resources of sugar from fruits and vegetables.

Although fruits & vegetables have organic sugars, also they provide many important nutrients such as vitamins, water, and fiber, which are advantageous to health.

Several Studies Also Show It Can Help You Shed Weight.

Plenty of proof suggests that the paleo diet works well for weight reduction. In one research, 14 healthy clinical college students were told to check out a paleo diet plan for three weeks.

During the research, they lost typically 5.1 lbs (2.3 kgs) and decreased their waistline circumference by 0.6 ins (1.5 cm). Interestingly, some research evaluating the paleo diet plan and traditional low-fat diet programs have found how the paleo diet works more effectively for weight reduction, even with comparable calorie intakes.

In one research, 70 obese women aged 60 and above followed the paleo diet plan or perhaps a low-fat, high-fiber diet plan for two years. Women around the paleo diet plan dropped 2.5 times more excess weight after half a year and 2 times more excess weight after a year.

From the two-year tag, both groups had regained a few pounds, however, the paleo group had nevertheless lost 1.6 times more excess weight overall.

Another study noticed 13 people with Type 2 diabetes who followed a paleo diet plan and a diabetes diet plan (low-fat and moderate-to-higher carb) for more than 2 consecutive three-months.

Normally, those in the paleo diet plan misplaced 6.6 lbs (3

kgs) and 1.6in (4 cm) even more using their waistlines than those for the diabetes diet plan. Unfortunately, most study in the paleo diet plan is fairly fresh. Thus, you can find very few released research on its long-term results.

It's also well worth noting that hardly any studies over the paleo diet plan compare its results on weight reduction to other diet plans' results on weight reduction. While studies claim that the paleo diet plan is superior, evaluating it to more diets would improve this argument.

It Improves Other Areas of Health

Along with its results on weight reduction, the paleo diet plan has been associated with many other health advantages.

May Reduce Stomach Fat

Belly fat is incredibly unhealthy and escalates the threat of diabetes, cardiovascular disease, and many other health issues. Studies show the fact that the paleo diet works well in reducing stomach fat. In one research, 10 healthy women followed a paleo diet plan for 5 weeks. Typically, they encountered a 3-in (8-cm) decrease in waistline circumference, which is a good indicator of stomach fat, and around the 10-lb (4.6-kg) weight reduction general.

May Boost Insulin Level of sensitivity and Reduce Blood Sugar Levels

Insulin sensitivity identifies how easily your tissues react to insulin. Upping your insulin sensitivity will be a good thing since it makes the body better at removing sugars from your blood vessels.

Studies have discovered that the paleo diet raises insulin level of sensitivity and lowers blood sugar levels. In two-week research, 24 obese people who have Type 2 diabetes followed the paleo diet or perhaps a diet with reasonable sodium, low-fat dairy, whole grains, and legumes.

By the end of the analysis, both groups encountered increased insulin awareness, but the results were stronger in the paleo team. Notably, only in the paleo team did those that were almost all insulin resistant encounter increased insulin level of sensitivity.

May Reduce Cardiovascular Disease Risk Factors

A paleo diet is fairly similar to diet programs recommended to market heart health.

It's lower in sodium and encourages slim sources of proteins, healthy body fat, and fruits and vegetables. That's exactly why it's zero coincidence that research has shown a paleo diet plan may reduce danger factors associated with cardiovascular disease, including:

Blood circulation pressure: A good analysis of 4 research with 159, most people discovered that a paleo diet plan reduced systolic blood circulation pressure by 3.64mmHg and diastolic blood circulation pressure by 2.48mmHg, normally.

Triglycerides: Several researches has discovered that eating the paleo diet plan could reduce overall bloodstream triglycerides by around 44%.

LDL cholesterol: Several studies have discovered that eating a paleo diet plan could reduce "poor" LDL cholesterol by around 36%.

Might Reduce Inflammation

Inflammation is an organic process that help your body

heal and battle infections. Nevertheless, chronic inflammation will be harmful and may increase the threat of illnesses like cardiovascular disease and diabetes.

The paleo diet plan emphasizes food items that will help reduce chronic inflammation. It promotes feeding on fruits and veggies, which are excellent resources of antioxidants. Antioxidants help, bind, and neutralize free of charge radicals in the torso that damage tissue during chronic swelling.

The paleo diet plan also recommends fish as a way to get protein. Fish will be abundant with omega-3 essential fatty acids, which may decrease chronic irritation by suppressing bodily hormones that promote chronic swelling, which includes TNF-α, IL-1, and IL-6

Ideas to Maximize Weight Reduction on

the Paleo Diet

If you'd prefer to get one of this paleo diet, here are some tips to help you shed weight:

Eat more vegetables: They're low in calorie consumption and contain fiber, helping you to stay whole for longer.

Eat several fruits: Fruit is nutritious and intensely filling. Try to consume 2-5 pieces each day.

Prepare beforehand: Prevent temptation by planning several meals to help you through busy times.

Get a lot of rest: The good night's rest might help you get rid of fat by maintaining your fat-burning hormones normal.

Stay active: Regular physical exercise helps burn up extra calories to improve weight loss.

It's popular that carrying out a paleo diet plan might help you shed weight.

It's saturated in protein, lower in carbs, might reduce the urge for food, and eliminates ready-made food items and added sugars.

If you don't like keeping track of calories, proof suggests a paleo diet plan is a great option.

However, you must remember that the paleo diet may not be for everyone. For example, those that have a problem with food limitation could find it hard adapting to the options around the paleo diet.

CHAPTER 6

Paleo Diet Plan Meal Strategy: A Straightforward Manual

The paleo diet plan is a diet program that mimics how pre-historic people could have eaten. It entails consuming whole food items that people could search or collect.

Promoters from the paleo diet plan decline contemporary diet programs that are usually filled with processed food items. They think that time for how hunter-gatherers consumed could cause less health issues.

The paleo diet plan isn't safe for everybody. Physicians have no idea of its results on kids, women that are pregnant, or old grownups. Individuals with persistent problems, such as inflammatory intestinal illness, should furthermore talk to a physician before trying a paleo diet plan.

This manual explores paleo principles and a 7-day paleo diet meal intend to follow. Continue reading to understand how to consume like our forefathers.

The focus of the paleo diet plan is on eating foodstuffs that might have already been obtainable in the Paleolithic era. The paleo diet plan will be furthermore referred to as the rock age group diet plan, hunter-gatherer diet plan, or caveman diet plan.

Before contemporary agriculture developed around 10,000 years back, people usually ate foods they could hunt or gather, such as fish, liver organ, fruits, vegetables, peanuts, and seeds.

The introduction of contemporary farming changed how people ate. Milk products, dried beans, and grains grew to become a section of people's diet plans.

Advocates from the paleo diet plan believe that the body hasn't evolved to procedure dairy products, dried beans, and grains that feed on these food types could raise the threat of certain health issues, such as cardiovascular disease, being overweight, and diabetes.

7-days paleo diet meal plan

We've created a 7-days paleo diet plan meal program with the purpose of providing helpful information for those who want to try out this method of feeding on paleo.

Individuals could make modifications to each food following their individual choice. Fruit, nut products, and seed products create outstanding snack foods or sweets.

Day 1

On the initial day, an individual could consume the following:

Breakfast: Avocado, kale, banana, and apple healthy smoothie with almond dairy.

Lunch: Mixed greens results with fried seabass, pumpkin seed products, and good essential olive oil.

Supper: Roast poultry having a filling of onions, celery, and rosemary.

Day 2

On the next day, utilize the leftover spots for lunch and revel in catch dinner:

Morning meal: Scrambled eggs with wilted spinach, grilled tomato vegetables, and pumpkin seed products.

Lunch: Mixed greens results with remaining roast poultry and a good essential olive oil outfitting.

Supper: Oven-baked trout with asparagus and broccoli fried in coconut essential oil.

Day time 3

On-day 3, use any remaining trout from the prior day time:

Breakfast: Chopped plums with blueberries and almonds.

Lunch: Mixed greens results in with remaining trout and a good olive essential oil.

Supper: Meat stir-fry with combined peppers, making use of coconut essential oil to fry.

Day 4

Around the fourth day, focus on a protein-packed egg:

Breakfast: Broccoli fried in coconut essential oil with toasted almonds along with a poached egg.

Lunch: Mixed greens with tuna, boiled eggs, seed products, and essential olive oil.

Supper: Harissa-baked poultry wings with steamed

broccoli.

Day time 5

On Day 5, an individual could prepare the following:

Morning meal: Coconut whole milk, mixed fruits, and spinach juice smoothie.

Lunch: Butternut lead pages, broccoli, and tomato omelet with mixed greens.

Supper: Crimson pepper, broccoli, child hammer toe, and trout stir-fry.

Day 6

In the sixth day, focus on a savory breakfast:

Breakfast: Bacon, eggs, and tomato vegetables fried in essential olive oil.

Lunch: Mixed veggie and poultry soups with turmeric.

Supper: Grilled lamb chops with wilted spinach and spiced crimson cabbage.

Day time 7

On day 7, add healthful body fat through the use of avocado:

Breakfast: Springtime onion, tomato, and mushroom omelet.

Lunch: Mixed greens with poultry, avocado, seed products, and essential olive oil.

Supper: Slow-cooked meat stew with blended veggies.

Health advantages of paleo

Individuals declare that the paleo diet plan gives numerous health advantages, such as promoting weight reduction, reducing the chance of diabetes, and decreasing blood pressure.

In this area, we go through the scientific evidence to find out what the study facilitates these claims:

Excess weight loss

A mature 2008 research discovered that 14 healthy volunteers achieved the average weight reduction of 2.3 kilos by following a paleo diet plan for 3 several weeks.

In 2009, researchers compared the consequences from the paleo diet plan having a diet plan for diabetes on 13 people who have type 2 diabetes. The little research discovered that consuming the paleo method decreased individuals' body weight and waistline area.

The 2014 research of 70 post-menopausal ladies with weight problems discovered that carrying out a paleo diet plan helped individuals shed weight after six months.

Nevertheless, right after 24 months, presently there has been simply no difference in weight reduction among individuals following a paleo diet and the ones sticking with regular Nordic nutritional suggestions. These outcomes claim that some other healthy diet programs could be simply as effective at advertising weight reduction.

The authors of the 2017 review noted that this paleo diet plan helped reduce weight for a while but figured this result is because of caloric restriction or consuming fewer calories.

Generally, the study shows that the paleo diet plan can help people shed weight initially but that additional diet plans that reduce calorie consumption might end up being effective.

Even more, study is essential before physicians recommend the paleo diet plan for weight reduction.

Presently, physicians recommend visitors to follow a calorie-controlled exercise and diet even more to lose excess weight.

Decreasing diabetes risk

Carrying out a paleo diet program reduce one's danger of building diabetes? The outcomes of some preliminary research are usually encouraging.

Insulin level of resistance is a dangerous element for diabetes. Improving one's insulin level of sensitivity reduces the probability that they can lead to diabetes and may help those people who have diabetes decrease their signs and symptoms.

A study in 2015 compared the consequences from the paleo diet plan with those of a diet plan predicated on recommendations from your American Diabetes Association on people who have type 2 diabetes.

While both diet programs improved the individuals' metabolic health, the paleo diet plan was better at improving insulin level of resistance and blood sugar levels control.

A 2009 research of nine sedentary volunteers without obesity furthermore discovered that the paleo diet plan improved insulin awareness.

There's a requirement for a more recent study for the paleo diet plan and diabetes, however, the evidence up to now shows that eating just like a hunter-gatherer may improve insulin sensitivity.

Decreasing blood circulation pressure

Increased blood pressure is a risk factor for cardiovascular disease. Many people believe that the paleo diet plan can help maintain bloodstream pressure in balance and advertise coronary heart wellness.

A 2008 research of 14 healthy volunteers discovered that following a paleo diet plan for 3 weeks improved systolic blood circulation pressure. It furthermore reduced excess weight and whole body bulk catalog (BMI). The analysis does not add a handle team, nevertheless, therefore the outcomes are usually not conclusive.

The 2014 research supported these early results. Experts in comparing the consequences from the paleo diet plan with those of a diet plan the Nederlander Wellness Authorities recommend on 34 individuals with features of metabolic symptoms, a disorder that escalates the danger of cardiovascular disease.

Outcomes showed how the paleo diet plan reduced blood circulation pressure and bloodstream lipid user profile, both of which may improve center wellness.

Although preliminary studies claim that the paleo diet may reduce blood circulation pressure and support heart health, newer and considerable studies are essential to create any conclusions.

Acknowledgments

The Glory of this book success goes to God Almighty and my beautiful Family, Fans, Readers & well-wishers, Customers, and Friends for their endless support and encouragement.

CPSIA information can be obtained
at www.ICGtesting.com
Printed in the USA
BVHW040450280321
603587BV00009B/2839

9 781954 634848